# shalom!

## CELTIC PRAYERS for WHOLENESS and HEALING

# shalom!

## CELTIC PRAYERS *for* WHOLENESS *and* HEALING

# RAY SIMPSON

Copyright © 2024, Anamchara Books.

All rights reserved. No part of this publication may be reproduced or transmitted for commercial purposes, except for brief quotations, without written permission of the publisher. Churches and other noncommercial interests may reproduce portions of this book without the express written permission of Anamchara Books, provided that the text does not exceed 500 words or 5 percent of the entire book, whichever is less, and that the text is not material quoted from another publisher. When reproducing text from this book, include the following credit line: "From *Shalom!: Celtic Prayers for Wholeness and Healing*, published by Anamchara Books. Used by permission."

Vestal, New York 13850

www.AnamcharaBooks.com

paperback ISBN: 978-1-62524-906-7

eBook ISBN: 978-1-62524-907-4

*Eternal Source of Life, you are the core of our being.*
*Flow through our bodies like a life-giving river.*
*Wash and transform the negative conditions*
*in our hearts, minds, bodies, and circumstances*
*with light, love, and grace.*

# CONTENTS

Introduction ........................................... 9

I. Blessings for Wholeness & Healing ......... 17

II. Physical Health .................................. 37

III. Psychological Well-Being .................. 47

IV. Spiritual Completion ........................ 67

V. World Harmony .................................. 91

# INTRODUCTION

The title of this book—*Shalom: Celtic Prayers for Wholeness and Healing*—contains three words that may need to be defined: *shalom, Celtic,* and *prayer.*

## Shalom

You might think that a book with this title should mention "peace" in the subtitle, since most of us have heard that *shalom* is the Hebrew word that means "peace." We read verses like this one—"You will keep in perfect peace [shalom] those whose minds are steadfast, because they trust in you" (Isaiah 26:3)—and we think we know what the author meant when he wrote *shalom*. Actually, though, the reality that Isaiah had in mind was quite different from our modern-day understanding of "peace."

According to an online dictionary, peace can be defined as: (1) freedom from disturbance; (2) the absence of war. This concept of peace is defined by what it is *not*.

By contrast, *shalom* is defined by what it *is*: completeness, wholeness, well-being, safety, prosperity, contentment, health, friendliness, wellness, rest, ease. All those qualities are wrapped up in that one small word. It implies the divinely ordained state of well-being, of justice, equity, and fulfilment, which God wants for each of us as individuals and for all of us as communities. It is a state of harmony, an interwoven connection that supports and nourishes both the parts and the whole.

God wants us whole... complete. God yearns to heal what is wounded or diseased, restore what is lost, and mend what is broken. This is the work of Christ, reconciling all Creation with Divinity, so that we all enter and participate in *shalom*.

We need *shalom* in our bodies, our minds, and our spirits—and we need it in our relationships and in our communities. For that reason a section of this book is devoted to each of these categories:

- physical health
- psychological well-being
- spiritual completeness
- world harmony

(The book also has another section, focused on a specific type of prayer, but we'll talk about that a bit later.)

Keep in mind, though, that for the Celts, these four divisions would not have existed. They would not have separated physical health from psychological and spiritual, and they recognized far more than we do today that individual well-being and community health are so interwoven as to be practically inseparable.

## Celtic

Why does the word *Celtic* describe the prayers in this book? Well, for several reasons, at various levels.

First, the Celtic expression of Christianity in the early Middle Ages is the indigenous Christianity of the English-speaking world—and, as church historian Henry Chadwick said, "Any church or nation that forgets its memory becomes senile." Scripture frequently calls us to remember God-guided pioneers such as Abraham, Israel, and Moses, and the "rock from which we were quarried" (Isaiah 51:1). The story of the pioneers who first evangelized Celtic lands might be regarded as The Acts of the Apostles Book Two.

Second, Ray Simpson believes that many models of church and mission have been defective. Celtic Christianity offers us a better model for today. Previous models were influenced by Greek dualism that separates spirit from matter. The Celtic model, like the Hebrew, is holistic. In addition to that, most expressions of church have been top-down, either allied to empires and states, or started independently by talented individuals who have not put to death an empire-building mentality. The typical early Celtic model of church is bottom-up, not top-down. It is incarnational, Earth-honoring, rooted in spiritual disciplines that sustain humility, community, and service.

But we need to go back yet another level and explain *who* the Celts were. The term is used differently by archaeologists, historians, and researchers of social and spiritual phenomena. Some academics would even say that the Celts never were a distinct people at all. But for our purposes, we are speaking about the people who lived in the insular lands—Ireland, Scotland, England, Wales, and Brittany—during the fifth to eighth centuries, as well as the centuries that followed with the varied expressions of their spiritual beliefs.

Although some scholars are keen to point out that early churches in Celtic kingdoms were part of the "one, holy, catholic and apostolic church" throughout the world, certain Gospel qualities shine especially brightly in the Celtic tradition. Among these was an informal style of prayer; an awareness that the presence of Christ, angels, and heaven could break into ordinary life; a belief in Divine healing; and a spiritual sense of place that led to "the healing of the land."

## Prayer

You might think this word is self-evident, but let's look at Celtic prayer in particular. We have a rich history of recorded prayers, going back to ancient Irish writings and including the *Carmina Gadelica,* published at the beginning of the twentieth century. These prayers have certain things in common: a sense of poetry, the prayerful repetition of phrases and words, a love of the Trinity, an absolute trust in both Divine power and Divine love, and a sense of compassion for self and others.

Prayer is, by definition, a form of communication with the Divine. Prayer can be wordless: the "groanings too deep for words," the companionable silence of friends, or the hushed intimacy of lovers. But Celtic prayers have words, for the Celts believed in the power of words to shape reality. They believed with such confidence that looking back from our position in the twenty-first century, we might say that for the Celts (both Pagan and Christian), words were magic. However, modern scientific research has proven the power of verbal affirmations to shape brain chemistry, aid in decision-making, and boost creativity—and as followers of Christ, we believe that through prayer, we somehow participate in the Spirit's work. In other words, this is "magic" only in the sense that something mysterious is going on behind the scenes when we pray, something we don't fully understand and yet something we can come, with practice, to utterly rely upon.

In the first section of this book, we have gathered a particular kind of prayer: blessings. These prayers are intended to be said out loud, in the presence of one or more other human beings. As you pray these prayers, you may want to lay your hands on the person for whom you are praying. You might want to anoint with oil. We've also included in this section a particularly Celtic blessing called the *caim* or *encircling prayer*. For these prayers, you use your finger to draw an invisible circle around you and whoever else is present and participating in the prayer. This circle represents a spiritual barrier that shields all that is healthy and life-giving, while preventing anything that is destructive or harmful from entering. The Celts believed that not only was the Trinity present and powerful, but also that hosts of angles were everywhere, ready to aid and help us.

In *The Celtic Way of Prayer*, Esther de Waal writes:

> I have come to see that the Celtic way of prayer is prayer with the whole of myself, a totality of praying that embraces the fullness of my own personhood and allows me not only to pray with words but also, more important, with the heart, the feelings, using image and symbol, touching the springs of my imagination.

The prayers in this book are Ray Simpson's, written from his heart with "the whole" of himself. And now his prayers are yours. May they allow you also to pray with your entire being, the "fullness of your personhood," "touching the springs of your imagination." May they guide you into the *shalom* of Christ.

*May the Divine Creator*
*make us instruments of healing.*
*May the Complete Christ*
*take from us all that frustrates healing.*
*May the Holy Spirit*
*give us power for healing.*

# 1

# BLESSINGS
# FOR WHOLENESS
# & HEALING

*The healing rhythm of the Trinity:*

We lift up ———,
in the eye of God,
in the love of Jesus,
in the name of Spirit,
in Trinity of power.
May ——— be healed.

May this water be for your healing
in the holy name of the Creator,
in the holy name of Jesus,
in the holy name of the Spirit,
in the holy name of the Three,
everlasting, kindly, wise.

May you be
lit by the glory of God,
drawn by the light of God,
warmed by the fire of God,
healed by the love of God.

Jesus who stopped the wind and stilled the waves,
grant you calm in the storm times;
Jesus, victor over death and destruction,
bring safety on your voyage;
Jesus of the purest love, perfect companion,
bring guarding ones around you;
Jesus of the miraculous catching of fish
and the perfect lakeside meal,
guide you finally ashore.
Jesus of the healing hands,
bring wholeness to every broken part.

*When a person suffers from insecurity or a lack of identity*

An eye was seeing you,
a mouth has named you,
a heart has thought of you,
a mind has desired you.

May Three Persons sanctify you,
May Three Persons help you,
the Creator and Christ and the perfect Spirit.

*A prayer for the removal from the body
of microbes or other unhealthy cells*

May God search them,
may God remove them
from your blood,
from your flesh,
from your urine,
from your smooth, fragrant bones;
from your close veins,
from your hard kidney,
from your pith, from your marrow, dear one,
from this day and every day,
till the day your life in this world
shall reach its end.

*For any skin or blood disease*

May God heal you, my dear one.
I am now placing my hand on you
in the name of Creator, Christ,
and Spirit of virtue,
Three Persons who encompass you for ever.
Full healing come to your blood,
perfect healing to your soft flesh,
another healing to your smooth skin,
in the name of the powers of the Holy Three.

*Prayer for an infected or injured eye
while bathing or touching it*

Pour, King of Life,
pour, Christ of Peace,
pour, Spirit of Cleansing.
You who created the orb
and placed the pupil in the eye,
search the mystery within the lid,
and befriend its sight, O God.
Make whole this day the eye;
restore this day the sight.

*Prayer for healing from any disease of the body*

May the strong Giver of Life
destroy your disease of body
from the crown of your head
to the base of your heel—
with the power of the Christ of Love
and the Creator of the seasons;
with the aid of the Holy Spirit
and the powers of wholeness together.

*For a swelling*

Peace come into this swelling,
the peace of the Ruler of Power.
Subsiding come to your swelling,
in the holy presence of the Creator,
in the holy presence of the Child,
in the holy presence of the Spirit,
the holy presence of compassion.
Look, O Christ, on this swelling.
Since you are the Giver of Life,
give rest to this person.
Bring all infection from this swollen area.
Be whole.
Let your swelling now shrink

*Prayer of healing after a miscarriage.*

The child who was lost through miscarriage
is not lost to you, Life-Giver.
We give this child the name ———.
We pray that you will heal
the scars of ———'s mother and father.
May ——— be enfolded in your love.
May ———'s parents find healing.
Set ——— free from all shock or hurt
that hinders her/his journey
into eternal wholeness in your kingdom,
so that ——— may live with you
in light and joy forever.
I look forward to that day when
we may all be reunited in paradise.

Healing Christ,
you walk the world with those who suffer
in broken places of the world.
We come to you with our wounds and theirs.
Encircle those for whom we pray.
Circle ———;
keep health within and harm without.
Circle ———;
keep wholeness within and pain without.
Enter their bodies, minds, and spirits.
And heal them of all that harms.

Circle this place by day and by night,
in winter's cold and summer's light.
Keep within Christ's healing balm;
keep without all that would harm.

Circle us, Life-Giver.
Keep trust within, keep fear without.
Keep love within, keep hate without.
Keep hope within, keep despair without.
Keep goodness within, keep evil without.
Keep healing within, keep illness without.
Keep wholeness within,
keep brokenness without.

Circle us, Healer of Our Souls.
Keep these evils without:
the evil of fear,
the evil of boasting,
the evil of pretense,
the evil of excess,
the evil of abuse.

Circle us, Healer of Our Lives.
Keep these good things within:
    the goodness of courage,
    the goodness of humility,
    the goodness of integrity,
    the goodness of simplicity,
    the goodness of kindness.

Circle this place, O God,
and keep these good things within
that we may each be healed:
eagerness to learn,
flowering of talents,
experience of beauty,
warmth of friendship,
respect for all,
care for the planet.

Circle this place, O God,
and keep these bad things without
that we may all be healed:
low self-esteem,
confusion, prejudice,
pride, stealing, fear.

# physical health

We are appealing to you,
since you are the Ruler of Heaven.
We are praying to you,
since you are the Giver of All Good.
Lift each wasting,
each weariness and sickness.
Lift each soreness and discomfort.
We are urgently praying to you.
Lift each stiffness,
as you separate earth from ocean.

God of Rest,
come as dew
that rests on our tired frames.
Come as breeze
that cools in the heat of the day.
Come as the calming presence
that restores stillness to our being.
Come as Sabbath rest
and renew our being.
Heal our bodies
and heal our souls.

In your presence,
we affirm that every organ,
action, and function of our bodies
is animated by your living Spirit.
By day and by night
may your Life flowing through us
renew every cell of our bodies
after your indwelling image.

*Prayer for infertility*

Call forth life within us,
Creator of Life.
Bless the swarming sperm
that teems with life so manifold.
Spirit of Life,
bless the welcoming egg
that patiently waits to conceive.
Savior of Life,
change the water of this womb
into a wine-like ferment of life.
Call forth life within us.

God make us fit for purpose,
alive in heart and limb.
God stretch our creaking bodies
till they tingle and feel trim.

Put fiber in our being,
take flabbiness away.
Strengthen what is weak,
keep binge and bulge at bay.

May each body be a temple
of your Spirit who is true;
a picture frame on earth
of eternity on view.

Grant us grace to
eat well,
think well
and move well,
until our bodies
are truly temples of your Holy Spirit.

Jesus, you healed a mother of her sickness:
heal those who have caught an infection.
Jesus, you restored a woman who was bleeding:
restore all those who bear
wounds that will not heal.
Jesus, you raised the dead:
raise up those who have been
struck down by illness.

God of wholeness,
may our hospitals not be centers of disease
but centers of healing.
May they not treat cases but help people.
May nurses and doctors,
cleaners and chaplains,
administrators and ambulance drivers
increase their compassion.
May many people grow well,
while others die well,
and staff work well.
Through Christ the Great Physician,
who heals us all and makes us whole.

# psychological
# well-being

As Christ removed the sleep
from the little child of the grave,
may he remove from you, dear one,
each frown, each envy, each malice.

Risen Christ, you turned Mary's tears into joy;
turn our tears into joy.
Risen Christ, you turned the
travelers' despair into hope;
turn our despair into hope.
Risen Christ, you turned the
disciples' fears into boldness;
turn our fears into boldness.
Risen Christ, you turned
an empty catch into fullness;
turn our empty routines into fullness.
Risen Christ, you turned Thomas's
unbelief into trust;
turn our unbelief into trust.
Risen Christ, by your wounds we are healed;
make our broken hearts whole.

Christ who stilled the storm,
still the turmoil within this heart.
Christ who overcame ill,
may no evil take root.

Come, O Spirit of Love
that goes to any lengths,
that breaks through a lifetime's crippling habits,
that wells up from the depths.
Come, O Spirit of Joy
that brings a song into haggard lives,
a serenity into our roots,
and a sparkle into our eyes.
Come, O Spirit of Peace
that heals mistrust
and brings us into harmony
with the still center of the universe.
Come, O Spirit of Kindness
that delights to sweeten the lives of others
and do beautiful things for God.

Come, O Spirit of Goodness
that opens the heart to Christ
in friend and stranger.
Come, O Spirit of Gentleness
that bears all things without
harshness or hardness.
Come, O Spirit of Fire
that burns away lust and double-minded ways.
Come, O Spirit of Wisdom
that teaches us to see into the nature of things
in order to know, speak, and do what is right.
Come, O Spirit of Power
that snaps the chains of fear
and casts out the demons of hell and hopelessness.
Make us whole.

Give us your firelight, Holy Spirit,
as we go down into the things
stored in our memories,
the dreams and hurts.
Journey with us beyond these
to the seed of our nature you planted in us
at our beginning.
May we become that seed,
which is our true self,
and may it grow and produce much fruit.

Almighty God of the invincible force-field,
repel these alien mind-invaders.
Disarm these hidden persuaders.
Evaporate these false imaginations,
and fill with your loving fragrance
the places they vacate.

We pray for the cleansing of our perceptions,
that we may hear,
that we may see,
that we may understand with our hearts
and that we may be healed.

Source of Love,
God of Compassion,
Bearer of our pain,
you accept what we hardly dare name.
You know all,
even more than we can recall.
May we find no part of Creation alien.
Embrace in your heart
what we have rejected in ourselves.
Your reflection is in our deepest core.
Flow through
every cranny of our being and our memory
like a pure, life-giving stream
that we may daily grow more whole.

Dear Father,
Mother,
Source of my being,
the precious robe with which you birthed me
is torn into shreds.
Love has been scattered.
Yet I long for you,
and you long to gather back together
the fragments of my life.
You know who I am.
Snatch me from the maze.
Restore me to my right mind.
Heal my wounds.
Return me to fellowship with the human family
and make me one with you.

Free me, Immense Spirit,
from a lifetime's crippling habits,
from a closed and cabined mind,
from a cowering, timid spirit,
from blinkered, haughty habits,
to be who I am,
clothed and in my right mind.

Life-Giver, sometimes I feel beaten and battered.
I ask you to fill more of your people
with compassion,
so that one of them will come alongside me.
I am lonely and sad.
I need a helping hand

God of tender, loving care,
bless us, your battered children.
Take the pain out of our lives.
Take the fear out of our lives.
Take the despair out of our lives.
Take the resentment out of our lives
and fill us with your gentle, healing love.

Bruised?

The blessing of acceptance be yours.

Bitter?

The blessing of forgiveness be yours.

Angry?

The blessing of gentleness be yours.

Suicidal?

The blessing of wise counsel be yours.

Broken?

The blessing of immortality be yours.

You came down
to lift us up.
You descended to Earth
that Earth might ascend to Heaven.
You descended to the dead
that the dead might rise to life.
Lift us up
from our fretting and our tiredness.
Lift us up
from disappointment.

Lift us, Life-Giver,
out of darkness into light,
out of despair into hope.
Lift us, Star-Birther,
out of sadness into joy,
out of failure into trust.
Lift us, Pain-Bearer,
out of anger into forgiveness,
out of pride into freedom,
and out of brokenness
into joyful well-being.

Great Spirit who broods over the world,
restore the garment of our self-respect
and remake us in your beauty.
Renew in us
the stillness of our being,
the soundness of our minds,
and bring to dawn our wholeness.
Heal us, we pray.

In each hidden thought our minds start to weave,
    be our canvas and our weaver.
In each wounded memory to which we cleave,
    be our counsel and our healer.

Help us, O Healing One,
to stop dwelling
on what others achieve that we don't.
As we look on the pattern in
the palm of each hand,
we thank you that each is uniquely personal.
May we grow in confidence, love, and creativity
according to the designs you have for us.
We forgive the ones who make us feel inferior.
Meet their needs; help them
find their best course.
Heal and have mercy on us all.

# SPIRITUAL COMPLETION

As we gaze into your light,
may the obedience of angels be ours;
may the joy of saints be ours;
may the humility of Mary be ours;
may the suffering of the cross be ours;
may the freeing of the bound spirits be ours;
may the glory of eternity be ours;
may the healing of the blind and broken
be ours, today and forever.

Three of Limitless Love,
may I fall into your lap.
I strain to be accepted
by people whose approval I desire.
I fear lest I go astray
or be left adrift on the ocean,
alone in a little boat named *Ego*.
You are always there,
inviting me to come in from the cold.
But I am conditioned to be stuck where I am.
Jesus, reach into my soul and place me
on the lap of the Three of Limitless Love,
where I can finally be healed.

We invite you, generous Healer,
into abandoned and wasted areas of our lives.
Visit these places with compassion.
Shine kindly and forgiving rays
of understanding upon them,
until the beauty that is within us
comes forth and our spirits sing again.
May we be lit by the glory of God,
filled with the health of God,
always tender and true.

Release in us the power of your Spirit
that our souls may be free to roam
your boundless stretches of space.
May we soar high like the eagle,
see horizons yet undreamed of,
glow with fires of compassion,
flow with streams of creativity.
Breath of God, blow away all that is unclean.
Breeze of God, refresh our tired frames.
Wind of God, blow us where you will.
Dew of God, refresh our tired routines.
Rain of God, revive our withered lives.
River of God, flow through us and heal our spirits.

Holy Raphael,
bring healing to those scarred by prejudice.
Holy Salathiel,
bring healing to those scarred by bad memories.
Holy Jegudiel,
bring healing to those scarred by fear of spirits.
Holy Barachiel,
bring healing to those scarred by fear of people.
Holy Jeremial,
bring healing to those scarred by mistreatment.
Holy Gabriel,
bring healing to those scarred by toxic religion.
Holy Michael,
bring healing to those scarred by war.

*Raphael is an archangel mentioned in the Book of Tobit and in 1 Enoch, whose name means "God has healed"; Christian tradition associates him with the angel who stirred the waters in the Pool of Bethesda (John 5:2–4). The Orthodox Church sees the archangel Salathiel as the patron saint of prayer and worship who helps people interpret dreams, break addictions, and protect children; people call on him when their spiritual lives suffer from distractions, inattentiveness, or coldness. Jegudiel is the archangel who is the advisor and defender of all who work in positions of responsibility to the glory of God; he is also known as the bearer of God's merciful love. Barachiel, which means "God has blessed," is considered to be the chief of the guardian angels and the patron saint of married people and families. Jeremiel, also known as Uriel, is the archangel of God's mercy; his job is to guide the deceased on their afterlife journeys. All these archangels' names come from books written between the Hebrew scriptures and the Christian, which Protestants consider to be apocryphal, but Catholic and Orthodox Christians accept as scripture. Gabriel, however, whose name means "man of God," is named in both the Book of Daniel and in the Gospel of Luke, and the Epistle of Jude and the Book of Revelation both mention the archangel Michael, the divine warrior, by name.*

Christ,
you are the refined molten metal
of our human forge.
Purge our desires,
strengthen our resolve,
sharpen our minds,
shape our wills,
heal our spirits.
Refine us
until we shine like you.

Saving Christ,

by your incarnation and birth in poverty,

set us free.

By your prayers and self-discipline,

set us free.

By your tender works of mercy,

set us free.

By your struggle for truth and justice,

set us free.

By your nobility in persecution,

set us free.

By the healing power of your touch,

set us free.

By your self-giving even in death

set us free.

Lead us from that which binds
to that which frees;
lead us from that which cramps
to that which creates;
lead us from that which lies
to that which speaks truth;
lead us from that which blights
to that which ennobles;
lead us from that which hides
to that which celebrates;
lead us from that which fades
to that which endures;
lead us from that which wounds
to that which heals.

O Holy Fire! O Holy Grace!
O overflowing Silent One!
By your birth, enable us;
by your overcoming of spirits,
arm us;
by your integrity, make us true;
by your fortitude in trials,
establish us;
by your self-giving in death,
change us;
by your mission to unquiet spirits,
raise us;
by your healing of the blind and bleeding,
crippled and cumbered,
make us whole.

Life-Giver, we leave behind with you
affections, habits, and attitudes that are
no part of a whole life.
This one thing we do:
we look to you and to the
fellowship of your sufferings
and to the power of your resurrection
and to the goal of the whole created universe—
becoming one with you.
So help us God.

You are the Well-Spring of Heaven,
the Fountain of Life.
Earth's springs of water,
green forests,
oceans and mountains,
are all doors into your presence.
In Nature, a way to you is opened.
Touch us. Refresh us. Heal us.
Flow over us and make us whole.

Thank you, Jesus, for your love for us;
for hurts you have healed
and faults you have changed;
for the thoughts you have inspired
and callings you have given.
May we share these joys as naturally
as we share the joys of a lovely day.

Thank you for the countless numbers
who have been made more whole through prayer.
Thank you for those who believe in themselves
for the first time.
Thank you for people of hate and violence
who now spread love and forgiveness.
Thank you for communities of hope
in an otherwise hopeless place.
Thank you that you work ceaselessly
to heal the human spirit.

Purify our lives like gold
that we may be royal priests to you.
Sanctify our hearts like incense
that we may be adorers of your presence.
Beautify our hearts like myrrh
that we may be your fragrance on Earth.
Heal our hearts like salve
that we may spread your healing love
to hurting spirits.

Jesus,
truly God, truly human,
truly infinite, truly frail,
your greatness holds the universe;
your face attracts our hearts;
your goodness beckons all that is good in us;
your wisdom searches us;
your truth reshapes us;
your generosity enriches our poverty;
your hand fills us with blessings;
your mercy brings forgiveness;
your love brings healing to our spirits.
Your glory fills the world.

Lead us into the desert of purging
that through reflection and prayer
we may leave behind the things
that tie our spirits down
and learn again to be your pilgrim people.
Through fasting from the frenzied
feeding of false desires,
through study of your word,
meditation, and acts of service,
restore the clearness of our seeing
and heal us to share your generous love with all.

O God, when the ride is bumpy
and the world passes us by,
you pour out your life for us,
right to the very end.
When we are edged aside
and doors are shut in our face,
you pour out your life for us,
right to the very end.
When others are out to get us
and our home is not secure,
you pour out your life for us,
right to the very end.
When our lives are but a flicker
in the darkness that encroaches,
you pour out your life for us,
right to the very end.
When our earthly lives are nearly over,
still you heal our spirits,
right to the very end.

The One who created us
came willingly to suffer for us;
let us spread our resolves before him
like branches of palm.
The Almighty comes to us
as one gentle and lowly of heart;
let us put on clothes of humility and praise.
The spirit is willing, but the flesh is weak;
let us watch and wait with him
that we may be healed.

Jesus, you taught that we
can only fulfill our calling
if we become like a seed that dies,
buried in the earth,
in order that many new ones may grow.
We break,
so that other may be healed.
We release our egos to the earth,
so that you may shine through us.

May we carry your cross
in our hearts through this day.
Your cross be in our eyes and in our looking.
Your cross be in our mouths and in our speaking.
Your cross be in our hands and in our working.
Your cross be in our minds and in our thinking.
May your cross bring healing and health
to all that we are and all that we do
today and every day.

You who lift the lowly and strengthen the frail,
who in your weakness raised a fallen world,
we thank you.
Lift each of us on to your shoulders
like a shepherd who does not
neglect one lost sheep.
Lift us from earth to heaven.
Heal all that is broken within our spirits
that we may be more like you.

# 5

# WORLD
# HARMONY

Life-Giver, today
may the needs of our bodies
and the needs of our minds
the practical needs of work
and the social needs
each be given their rightful place
and kept in balance.
May the needs for rest and fun,
study and sleep,
household order and justifiable work
all be answered.

You who order the universe,
pour your oil on the troubled waters of our lives.
We bring to you the troubles
in our places of work,
in our relationships,
in our church, and in the world.
Heal us, calm us,
and help us rest in you.

Creator,
we of this day are children of confusion:
restore the vision of God to us.
The noise of the city deafens us
to the still, small voice:
restore the hearing of God to us.
The pace of modern living deadens us:
restore the alertness of God to us.
The pride of fame and fashion enslaves us:
restore the liberty of God to us.

Divine Light encompassing us,
penetrate our souls, our minds, and our bodies.
Cleansing, healing soul-light,
shine out into our business dealings;
shine out into all dealings;
shine out into the architecture of life.

Break in us the drive to manipulate others;
embolden us to clear out the clutter;
inspire us to give all,
trusting that you will provide.

Lead us from wasting time
to making good use of time.
Lead us from showing off
to showing love.
Lead us from being unreal
to being real.

Help us to live simply
that others may simply live.
Free us from false attachments,
that we may be
true to ourselves,
true to others
and true to you.

Risen Christ, bring newness of life
into our stale routines,
into our wearied spirits,
into our tarnished relationships.

The glory of God in our working;
the glory of God in our thinking;
the glory of God in our speaking;
the glory of God in our eating;
the glory of God in our hearing;
the glory of God in our meeting.

Today's step:
we step away from fret,
we step toward rest.
We open our lives
to the healing of God.

We are children of confusion:
restore the vision of God to us.
The noise of the city
deafens us to the still, small voice:
restore the hearing of God to us.
The pace of modern living deadens us:
restore the alertness of God to us.
Reveal to us in our dreams
visions of your glorious truth.
Heal us and make us whole.

Holy God,
help us to live at the still center
of the world's whirring wheels,
where everything is led by you,
where all is one,
and we are at peace.

Restore to us, O God,
your rhythms that we have lost:
the rhythm of rising and sleeping;
the rhythm of rest and work;
the rhythm of breathing and walking;
the rhythm of quiet and speech;
the rhythm of loving and losing;
the rhythm of light and dark.

Gentle Father,
Life-Giving Mother,
bless all who suffer abuse:
children, elders, women,
and all who have been betrayed by those
whose job it is to care for them.
Take the hurt out of their lives.
May your gentle Spirit flow
through all those who care for them.
Heal ancient wounds.
Break the cycle of abuse.

God of Monday and of Sunday,
you have created a world
of limited natural resources;
and you have created humans
of limited duration and energy.
May we accept that we are mortal.
May we stop trying to be God.
May we live in a balance of input and output.

Teach us to leave behind
the things that tie our spirits down
and learn again to be your pilgrim people:
through fasting from
the frenzied feeding of false desires,
through study of your word,
meditation, and acts of service,
restore the clearness of our seeing
and free us, heal us
to share your generous love
with all.

God of Order and Beauty,
help us to clothe our bodies and our homes
with beauty appropriate to the season.
Give to us a sense of balance and of order,
with room for spontaneity.
Show us what bubbles and what brings calm,
what brings energy and what brings charm.

Open our eyes to the poisons of our time,

that we may avoid them.

Alert us to the angry horses of our time,

that we may calm them.

Prepare us for the prowling lions of our time,

that we may bring them to nothing.

Giver of all life
on Earth and in Heaven,
the food we eat is earth, water, and air,
coming to us through pleasing plants
or living creatures.
When we eat,
help us to keep these other lives in mind
and to keep it simple.

Divine Savior,
your birth in the stable at Bethlehem
reveals the simplicity of Divine love;
help us, like you,
to fling away burdensome accessories
and live in simplicity and joy.
Heal us from our need to hoard and hold.
May we, like you,
rest in stables and storm-tossed ships,
at peace with the world just as it is,
needing nothing more
than you.

Life-Giver, Pain-Bearer,
we offer you our tears for those broken by abuse
and our anguish for those who rebel against you.
We offer you the pain we endure
from those who are hostile
and our burdens for the needy and poor.
May our sufferings contribute to the suffering
that your universal body needs to complete
in order to transform
every last person and place on Earth.

In the strength of the Warrior of God,
I oppose all that pollutes.
In the eye of the Face of God,
I expose all that deceives.
In the energy of the Servant of God,
I bind up all that is broken.
Bring healing to our world.

We plead for your justice to fill all the lands
as the waters cover the sands.
We cry until our voices are sore.
We weep for the hungry and poor;
the children mistreated;
those broken by force;
and the wounded who can't finish their course.
We pray against cruelty, hatred, and pain;
against pride and greed for gain.
We pray for the homeless
and victims of war;
the strangers to love
who come to our door.

Where people long for an end to injustice,
shine into their hearts.
Where people long for conflict to cease,
shine into their hearts.
Where people long to right
inhuman working conditions,
shine into their hearts.
Where people long to restore
the scarred places of the Earth,
shine into their hearts.
Where people long for dignity
in human relationships,
shine into their hearts.

Great Creator,
we are made in your likeness,
and you call us to be co-creators with you.
Water the seeds of creativity
you have planted in us;
let not fear, over-busyness, or low self-image
hold us back from letting these come to flower.
May we, in a second-hand and sterile society,
be signs of your creative life.
May your creativity
flow through us
to remake and heal the world.

God, give us cities
where no one cheats,
where safe housing is available for all,
where internet use is free,
where stores sell affordable, healthy food,
where public transportation offers options,
where everyone can find meaningful work,
where clean water is plentiful,
and understanding thrives.
Show us the goals you have for our cities,
and give us wisdom and energy
to work with you
to make it so.

Generosity of God,
spilling over into Creation,
flow into us that we may
bless the air and the animals;
tend the Earth with care,
give love to your Creation
and live a rhythm that restores
well-being to the planet.

Generosity of God,
spilling over into Creation,
we bless you for flowers
and their wealth of beauty,
for creatures and their glorious variety,
for seas and seasons and scents;
may we, too, reflect
your boundless generosity,
so that love and healing
flow out from us
in every interaction.

When rich nations
begin to reap what they have sown,
may they learn from this to live more simply
that others may simply live,
to produce sustainably,
to invest ethically,
and to live as responsible members
of a world community.

May your presence draw people across the world
and reveal your mother-heart of compassion.
Pour into the world's empty cups
the beauty and blessings of Christ
and gather together your children.
You who became poor to make many rich:
transform our dullness with radiant light;
transform our drabness with vibrant joy;
transform our shallowness with
deepening wisdom;
transform our suffering with growing trust;
transform our wounds,
so that we work with you
to heal our world.

O Christ, you entered the stream of human life:
immerse us in the Divine life.
Immerse us in the waters that cleanse.
Immerse us in the waters that overwhelm evil.
Immerse us in the waters of creativity.
Immerse us in the waters of life everlasting.
Immerse us in the waters that heal
all that is broken in our world.

Teach us to leave behind
prejudice and meanness of spirit.
Incite us to generous giving.
Help us to create space for your Spirit
to work and build and heal.
Show us how to play our part
in the Realm of your love.

Christ of the scars,
into your hands we place
the broken, the wounded,
the hungry and the homeless,
the sick and alone.

Christ of the scars,
into your hands we place
those who have been betrayed or bereaved;
those who have suffered loss of limb or esteem,
family or friends, employment or home.
Christ of the scars,
into your hands we place
unwanted babies, children abused,
neighbors defamed, lovers spurned,
spouses deserted, elders forgotten.
Christ of the scars,
into your hands we place victims
of war and violence,
false accusation, or sharp practice.
Bring healing, we pray.

Jesus, as you are lifted up on a
tree placed in the Earth,
the rulers and empires of this world are exposed
for what they are—
cheap and short-lived substitutes
for true wholeness, true order,
true interconnection.
You are the way for true unity
in the human family;
all who are buried, humbled, and earthed
become your common ground,
the place where the nations are healed.
So may it be.

Jesus, before you left this Earth,
you urged us to immerse all people in your life.
We pray for parched and hungry people:
immerse them in your life.
We pray for torn and exiled people:
immerse them in your life.
We pray for lonely and unloved people:
immerse them in your life.
We pray for unjust and oppressive people:
immerse them in your life.
We pray for sick and hurting people;
immerse them in your life.
May the Eternal Glory shine upon us.
May the Son of Mary stay beside us.
May the life-giving Spirit work within us.
May we all be healed.

Spirit of God, among the wheels of industry,
renew the face of the Earth.
Spirit of God, among the computers of commerce,
renew the face of the Earth.
Spirit of God,
among crime-infested neighborhoods,
renew the face of the Earth.
Spirit of God, among tired and broken families,
renew the face of the Earth.
Spirit of God, among the lonely and the sick,
renew the face of the Earth.
Spirit of God, among the drugged
and disillusioned,
renew the face of the Earth.

*Prayer after terrorism.*

May those who are bereft of loved ones
after an act of terror
walk out their loss
and find a healing process.
May each one who died be replaced
by one who makes a new way of life.
As Nehemiah rebuilt the ruined city walls,
may we rebuild what is broken,
with God as our healing helper.

Jesus, you are the Healing Person,
the pattern of goodness,
the fulfilment of the highest human hopes,
the model that shows us how to live.
God who is with us, we adore you.


Jesus, you are the glory of eternity,
shining now among us,
the tenderness of God, here with us now.
God who is with us, we adore you.


Jesus, you are the champion of the weak,
the counsellor of the despairing,
the brother of us all.
God who is with us, we adore you.

Jesus, you are the splendor of the Creator,
the Son of Mary,
our Bridge between heaven and earth.
God who is with us, we adore you.

Jesus, you are the source of life,
the goal of the universe,
the people's friend, the world-pervading God.
God who is with us, we adore you.

Jesus, you are one of the human family,
Joy of Angels, Prince of Peace,
Healer of Nations,
God who is with us, we adore you.

May our churches bring honor to you
and healing to the people.
May they be places of hospitality and hope.
May they be seedbeds of justice and friendship.
May they be sanctuaries
for those who are oppressed.
May they bring refreshment
to tired traders and work people.
May they stir us to explore the endless adventure.
May they restore and bring new wholeness
to the world in which we live.

Holy Spirit,
breathe upon the cosmos.
May it share in Christ's resurrection
and grow with the birth pangs of his Realm.
May we, even in the middle
of its groanings and pains,
be instruments of its healing
and breathe peace upon it this day.

God, Source of our being,
we acknowledge that we are fragmented.
Our communities are suffering.
Give us courage to look at the wound
that lies at the heart of everything:
the wound we run away from,
the wound we hardly dare name.
May failures be forgiven,
wounds be healed,
confusions be resolved,
ignorance be dispelled,
relationships be treasured.

Spirit of Truth,
look down upon a world
in thrall to lies and illusions,
wounded by hatred,
diseased with selfishness.
Work in the darkness
to bring all things into light.
In the name of the God of wholeness,
in the name of Compassion's Son,
in the name of the healing Spirit,
tonight may we be one.

More books on Celtic
spirituality that are
also by Ray Simpson . . .


(All are available from Anamchara Books.
Amazon, and most online booksellers.)

# Celtic Christianity
## *Deep Roots for a Modern Faith*

The world of the long-ago Celts appeals to many of us in the twenty-first century. Whether we are looking to find our cultural heritage or are seeking an alternative to worn and restrictive religious forms, the earth-centered, woman-friendly, inclusive faith of the Christian Celts offers us a deep-rooted alternative approach to traditional Christianity. The Celts experienced "thin places," where they sensed the supernatural world; they honored their poets, singers, and artists; and they passionately followed the Christ of the Gospels. Theirs was a church without walls, which lived naturally and comfortably within the community. Ray Simpson has spent most of his life walking in the footsteps of the Christian Celts, and now he allows us to experience for ourselves their dynamic spirituality.

# The Celtic Book of Days

## *Ancient Wisdom for Each Day of the Year from the Celtic Followers of Christ*

The ancient Celts found God's presence in each ordinary moment of the day. Everything they encountered revealed to them the presence of the sacred; each day was deep with meaning. Now you too can practice the Celts' faith, as you take a few moments to immerse yourself in their wisdom. These small daily moments of reflection and insight will open your heart to each day and all it holds.

This day I call to me

God's strength to direct me,

God's power to sustain me,

God's wisdom to guide me. . . .

God's sheild to protect me.

*(Saint Patrick)*

# Celtic Prayers for
# the Rhythm of Each Day

We sometimes think prayer belongs only in certain places on certain days. This book calls us to set prayer free from these constraints, allowing it to flow out through the hours of every workday, sanctifying the ordinary rhythm of our modern lives: waking up, going to work, breaking for lunch, ending the workday, the evening hours, and going to bed.

Ray Simpson gives us twenty original prayers, written in the Celtic tradition or patterned after ancient Celtic prayers, for each of these intervals. Like generations of earlier followers of Christ, we too can use prayer to bless the rhythm of our daily lives, infusing the hours with the awareness of the One who gives us Life. These small pauses throughout the day will make us ever more aware that the Kingdom of Heaven is a constant and present reality, hidden just beneath the veil of everyday life.

# Tree of Life
## *Celtic Prayers to the Universal Christ*

*Christ is the visible image of the invisible God. He existed before anything was created and is supreme over all creation, for through him God created everything. . . . He existed before anything else, and he holds all creation together.*

—Colossians 1:15–17

Like a vast, ever-growing Tree of Life, Christ—the expression of Divine love—expands endlessly throughout the universe. This is the perspective of ancient Celtic spirituality, and it is this concept that Ray Simpson reveals in his poem-prayers. Inspired by the traditional Celtic style of prayer, he gives words to our individual relationships with God. He speaks of the wonder, beauty, and love revealed through the Universal Christ, the Tree of Life that includes all that is. Each and everything in creation is sacred, for everything is a word of God—and we too are called to be God's words to our world.

AnamcharaBooks.com

www.ingramcontent.com/pod-product-compliance
Lightning Source LLC
Chambersburg PA
CBHW060530080526
44586CB00012B/683